# The Loch Ness Monster

## by Bradley Steffens

50346

Lucent Books, P.O. Box 289011, San Diego, CA 92198-9011

These and other titles are included in the Exploring the Unknown series:

Bigfoot
The Curse of Tutankhamen
The Extinction of the Dinosaurs
Haunted Houses
The Loch Ness Monster
UFO Abductions

**Library of Congress Cataloging-in-Publication Data**
Steffens, Bradley, 1956-
    The Loch Ness monster / Bradley Steffens.
        p.  cm.—(Exploring the unknown)
    Includes bibliographical references (p.      ) and index.
    ISBN 1-56006-159-6 (acid-free paper)
    1. Loch Ness monster—Juvenile literature.  [1. Loch Ness
monster. 2. Monsters.]  I. Title.  II. Series: Exploring the unknown
(San Diego, Calif.)
QL89.2.L6S88   1995
001.9'44—dc20                                                        94-2120
                                                                            CIP
                                                                            AC

# CONTENTS

PROLOGUE

Does Something Strange Live in Loch Ness?                5

CHAPTER 1

Gathering Information: What Have People
Seen in Loch Ness?                7

CHAPTER 2

Forming a Hypothesis: What Kind of Creature
Might Nessie Be?                17

CHAPTER 3

Testing the Hypothesis: What Have Scientists
Found in Loch Ness?                29

CHAPTER 4

Confirming the Tests: Has Any New Evidence
of Nessie Been Found?                37

EPILOGUE        The Search Continues                43

GLOSSARY                45
FOR FURTHER READING                46
WORKS CONSULTED                46
INDEX                47
ABOUT THE AUTHOR                48
PICTURE CREDITS                48

For Ezekiel,
whose love of wonders
inspired this book

*Saint Columba made the first recorded sighting of a water monster in Loch Ness.*

# Does Something Strange Live in Loch Ness?

L ate in the sixth century, a Christian missionary who was later known as Saint Columba stood on the shore of the river Ness, a river in northern Scotland. He needed to cross the river, but he had no boat. He saw one moored on the far bank of the river, however, so he ordered one of his followers to get it.

Saint Columba watched as a follower named Lugne Mocumin waded into the icy water and began to swim toward the distant shore. Suddenly, something strange happened. According to Saint Adamnan, Saint Columba's biographer, "A water monster . . . came up and rushed toward the man, roaring, with an open mouth." Alarmed, Saint Columba acted quickly:

> The Blessed Man raised his Holy Hand, invoked the name of God, made the sign of the cross, and commanded the terrible monster, saying, "Stop. Go no further. Do not touch that man. Go away quickly." Hearing the saint's voice, the monster fled, faster than it had come.

This was the first recorded sighting of a monster in or around the river Ness, but it was not the last. At least ten thousand people have reported seeing something strange in the river Ness and in a nearby lake known as Loch Ness.

According to experts who have studied these reports, most sightings of the monster actually arose from natural events. People had seen ordinary things like birds, fish, floating logs, or small waves. Many observers have been confused by the appearance of such objects in Loch Ness because the lake's water is very dark. It contains countless particles of decayed matter known as peat. These particles make the water appear dark brown, almost black. The dark waters reflect light oddly, causing everyday objects to look strange.

Other witnesses were not tricked by their eyes; instead, they wanted to trick others. They made up stories about the monster to fool people. Such fake sightings are known as hoaxes.

Although most sightings have had natural causes, a small portion remain a mystery. According to an expert named Roy Mackal, at least 250 reports cannot be fully explained. Mackal believes the people who made these reports have seen a creature unknown to science. Some people refer to this creature as the Loch Ness Monster. Others have given it a nickname. They call it Nessie.

In the last fifty years, many people have tried to answer the riddle of what is in Loch Ness. Some of these people have been scientists. They have tried to prove or disprove the existence of the Loch Ness Monster using a system known as the scientific method.

The scientific method has five steps: 1) stating the problem or question, 2) gathering information about the problem, 3) forming a hypothesis, or possible answer to the problem, 4) testing the hypothesis, and 5) confirming the test results.

Each chapter of this book will use one step in the scientific method to explore the mystery of Loch Ness. This prologue presents the first step of the scientific method. It states the problem: some people have seen unusual things in and around Loch Ness. It also asks the question: does something strange live in Loch Ness?

# CHAPTER 1

# Gathering Information: What Have People Seen in Loch Ness?

In the fifteen centuries since Saint Columba drove off the "water monster," many people in the Scottish highlands have seen a strange beast in Loch Ness. Stories about a creature lurking within Loch Ness were so common that the lake was known for centuries simply as *Loch na Beiste*, Gaelic for "Lake of the Beast." For generations, parents living around the lake warned their children to watch out for the "terrible water kelpie" (water sprite). They accepted the strange beast as a fact of life, and they rarely spoke of it to outsiders.

Visitors to the lake did not take sightings of the beast as calmly as the local people did. The outsiders often published accounts of what they had seen. One of the first sightings by outsiders was made by a squad of British soldiers who had arrived at Loch Ness in 1725 to build a road along the south shore. One day, the soldiers heard noises coming from the water. They looked up to see two creatures "as big as whales" swimming in the lake.

The modern era of Loch Ness sightings began with the building of another road in 1933. This road was built along the north shore of the lake. The workers used dynamite to blast their way through the rocky ground. Cascades of rocks tumbled down the steep hills and into the water below. Many people believe the blasting disturbed creatures living in the depths of the lake. Frightened or just curious, the beasts surfaced more often than usual. At least fifty people reported seeing them in 1933, and dozens more reported sightings in the following years.

One of the most famous sightings was made by Mr. and Mrs. John Mackay as they drove along the south shore of Loch Ness.

Mrs. Mackay saw a great churning in the waters and "two large black humps moving in a line." She shouted to her husband to stop the car. John MacKay pulled to the side of the road. Together, the Mackays watched a creature the size of a whale "rolling and plunging for fully a minute." They reported that it made waves "large enough to have been made by a passing steamer [steamship]."

On April 20, 1933, the Mackays told a friend, Alex Campbell, what they had seen. Campbell, a fishing warden, told the Mackays that he had seen a similar creature "many times." Campbell decided to write a news story about the Mackay sighting. He did not use the Mackays' names, since they did not wish to be identified. On May 2, 1933, the *Inverness Courier* carried Campbell's report, entitled "A Strange Spectacle on Loch Ness." The Loch Ness Monster was no longer a secret.

*Mr. and Mrs. John Mackay watched a creature the size of a whale "rolling and plunging" in the waters of Loch Ness in 1933.*

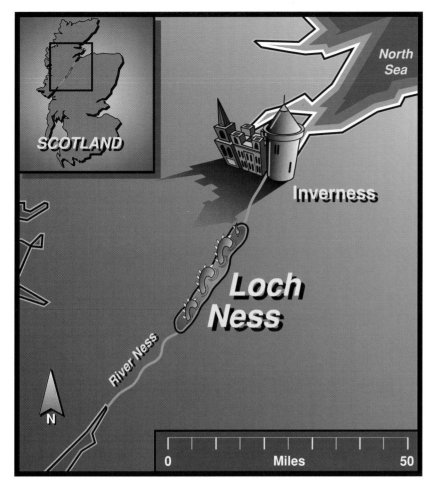

*Loch Ness is located in northern Scotland near the town of Inverness. The long, narrow lake lies roughly in the middle of the country, in a hilly area known as the Highlands. Twenty-four miles long and two miles wide, Loch Ness is the largest freshwater lake in Great Britain. Loch Ness empties into the river Ness, which flows into the North Sea. In this way, Loch Ness is connected to the ocean. For this reason, some people believe that the Loch Ness Monster is an ocean creature that has managed to swim up the river Ness and into the lake.*

## "A Loathsome Thing"

Two months after Campbell's news story appeared, Mr. and Mrs. George Spicer of London were driving along the same road from which the Mackays had observed the water beast. The Spicers, too, saw something strange. It was not in the water, however. It was on land, crossing the road in front of them.

Mr. Spicer slammed on the brakes. The creature "looked sort of like a giant snail with a long neck," Mr. Spicer later told reporters. Mrs. Spicer agreed, adding, "It was a loathsome thing. It was simply horrible." The hulking beast bounded across the road, down the hillside, and into the water. News about the Spicer sighting flashed around the world. Nessie, as the creature was nicknamed, was becoming famous.

Despite the Spicers' sworn statements and other reports about the lake creature, many people doubted the stories coming

# Why Is Loch Ness a Good Place to Hide?

If you were a large water animal looking for a good place to hide, you could not find a better place than Loch Ness. It is deep, dark, and filled with caves.

Loch Ness is located over an earthquake fault line, a deep crack in the earth's surface. As a result, it is one of the deepest lakes in the world. It is 925 feet deep in some places.

Thousands of years ago, the bottom of the lake was scoured by glaciers. The slow-moving ice carved the lake's rocky sides, leaving many caves and shelves. Sheltered by the rock, underwater creatures can escape even from the sonar waves sent down by Nessie hunters.

At the bottom of Loch Ness is a layer of decaying matter known as peat. Like coal, peat consists of carbonized vegetable matter, mostly moss. Floating peat particles make the water of Loch Ness dark brown, almost black. As a result, it is difficult to see through the water. Scuba divers and submarines are almost useless in the dark waters. The particles in the water make searching for Nessie difficult, if not impossible.

from Loch Ness. The skeptics, or doubters, wanted physical proof that the creature existed. A body, a track, or a photograph would help.

The world did not have to wait long for one of these.

## Photographic Evidence

On November 12, 1933, Hugh Gray, a farmer who lived beside Loch Ness, was out walking. In his hands he carried a simple box camera. Suddenly Gray noticed "an object of considerable dimensions, rising two or three feet above the water, dark grey in color with a smooth and glistening skin." Gray took five snapshots of the strange object. Later, Gray was disappointed to find that four of the pictures showed nothing. The fifth, however, revealed an unusual shape in the water. It was curving and "wormlike," narrow at one end and blunt at the other. This was the first photographic evidence of something unusual in Loch Ness.

*The first photograph of an object believed to be the Loch Ness Monster was taken by Hugh Gray, a farmer, on November 12, 1933. Gray's picture remains unexplained.*

Many people thought that Gray's photograph was too vague to be proof of anything. "My personal opinion," said one expert from the British Museum of Natural History, "is that [Gray's picture] shows a rotting tree trunk."

Then, in December, new evidence appeared that seemed to support Gray's claim that he had indeed seen the mysterious creature of Loch Ness. The English newspaper *The Daily Mail* reported that an African big-game hunter had found proof that the Loch Ness beast was real. Marmaduke Wetherell, the hunter, had found the creature's footprints.

From his experience tracking animals, he said, he could tell several things about Nessie. First, Nessie was an animal not presently known to scientists. Second, the animal was about twenty feet long. Third, like a crocodile, it could breathe air just by lifting its nostrils out of the water. Finally, because the tracks were only a few hours old, he knew it was alive and well and could not only swim, but walk.

Wetherell's report stirred great interest. Scientists made plaster casts of the tracks and sent them to the British Museum of Natural History. Tourists filled the local hotels and participated in "monster-hunting parties." A circus offered a reward of nearly $40,000 to anyone who could bring in the beast—dead or alive.

Then came the results of the British Museum's study of the footprints: They were a hoax! All four footprints were identical, and they looked like those made by a hippopotamus.

It turned out that they had been made by an umbrella stand formed from a petrified hippopotamus's foot. A local resident owned the umbrella stand, but, because Wetherell was already back in Africa, no one knew whether he had been part of the hoax or had been fooled by it.

The hippopotamus-footprint hoax put Nessie's existence in doubt once again. Many people who had been excited by Hugh Gray's photograph now thought that it too was probably a fake. Many people now thought the whole idea of a mysterious monster in Loch Ness was a joke.

Even so, people continued to experience signs of Nessie. Two months after Gray took his photograph (a few weeks after the Wetherell hoax was exposed), a local veterinary student named Arthur Grant was motorcycling along Loch Ness. Without warning, a strange beast crossed the road in front of Grant. The motorcyclist nearly crashed but was able to stop short of the giant creature. Grant did not have a camera, so he made a drawing of the animal he saw. Its neck was long and slender, but its body was thick and round. It had flippers in front, like a walrus or seal. It was not one of these familiar animals, however. The veterinary student was certain of that.

The next day, students from Edinburgh College visited the site where Grant had seen the creature. They found several tracks along the bank of Loch Ness. The tracks appeared to have been made by flippers, not feet. Nessie was a water beast, the students agreed.

Three months later, Dr. Robert Wilson presented the *Daily Mail* with another photograph taken at Loch Ness. The doctor said he had noticed a disturbance on Loch Ness about a hundred yards from shore. According to his story, Dr. Wilson stopped his car and took a picture. The doctor's photograph shows a long-necked creature swimming in the lake. For decades, Wilson's photograph was considered the best picture ever taken of the Loch Ness Monster.

When people found out that Dr. Wilson had taken his photograph on April 1, 1934—April Fools' Day—many assumed that the picture was a hoax. It seems these people were right. In 1992, two researchers, Alastair Boyd and David Martin, spoke with Christian Spurling, the stepson of Marmaduke Wetherell. Spurling confessed that he built a model of the

*Arthur Grant nearly collided with a huge creature that was crossing the road beside Loch Ness in 1934. A veterinary student, Grant was unable to identify the creature he saw.*

*For sixty years, the "Surgeon's Photograph" was believed to be one of the clearest pictures ever taken of the Loch Ness Monster. In 1992, Christian Spurling confessed that he and his stepfather, Marmaduke Wetherell, had faked the famous photograph.*

famous beast for his stepfather by attaching a foot-long neck to a fourteen-inch toy submarine. Wetherell placed Spurling's model in Loch Ness and snapped the famous picture. According to Spurling's account, Wetherell passed the phony photograph to Dr. Wilson to give to the *Daily Mail.*

The "Surgeon's Photograph" caused a sensation when it appeared in the April 21, 1934, issue of the *Daily Mail.* Showing a creature with a thick body and a long neck, the picture seemed to confirm the accounts given by the Mackays, the Spicers, and Hugh Gray. Because the photograph had been submitted by a doctor, many people assumed the image genuine. Scientists around the world decided they could no longer ignore the findings. It was time to take the Loch Ness Monster seriously.

# CHAPTER 2

# Forming a Hypothesis: What Kind of Creature Might Nessie Be?

A hypothesis is an educated guess about an unexplained thing or event. When stories about an unknown creature in Loch Ness began to appear in 1933, scientists tried to guess what kind of animal the witnesses had seen. As more sightings have occurred over the years, scientists have added to the list of possible explanations.

The British soldiers who observed something strange in the lake in 1725 said the creatures they saw were "as big as whales." The Mackays said the creature they saw in 1933 was "rolling and plunging" like a whale. Other people have described the Loch Ness Monster as blowing a fine mist into the air, as whales do. Because of these reports, some scientists reasoned that a whale had swum into the river Ness from the North Sea, then made its way up the river and into Loch Ness.

Other scientists hypothesized that the eyewitnesses had seen porpoises that had gotten into the lake in the same way. A porpoise coming to the surface to breathe can look like a dark hump. Two or three porpoises swimming together could look like the black humps Mrs. Mackay reported seeing. Porpoises also spray mist from their breathing holes.

Seals, too, appear as dark humps when they surface to breathe. They swim quickly, as Nessie does. They are able to stay under water for long periods of time. They like cold water. Their heads are small, as Nessie's is said to be, and they stretch out their necks when seeking food. Unlike whales and porpoises, seals also move about on land, bounding along on their bellies like the creature the Spicers sighted. For these reasons, some scientists thought Nessie might be a seal. The elephant seal is large enough to qualify as a small Nessie, the scientists suggested.

The students who examined the area where Arthur Grant saw a strange creature believed that the tracks they found were made by a walrus. Walruses, too, swim quickly and like cold water. Some scientists believed walruses were likely candidates to explain the strange sightings.

A large, swimming mammal known as a sea cow matches the descriptions of Nessie in many ways. One kind of sea cow, known as Stellar's sea cow, has been known to grow up to thirty feet long and weigh as much as eight thousand pounds. Stellar's sea cow is believed to be extinct now, but other sea cows still exist. While their bodies are large, their heads are small, like Nessie's. Sea cows often float with their heads and tails down, forming a large hump in the water. Mother sea cows carry their babies on their backs. A baby sea cow clinging to its mother's back might look like a hump. Could Nessie be a sea cow?

*Many scientists have hypothesized that the Loch Ness Monster is an animal already known to science. Possible Nessie candidates: (clockwise from bottom) sea lions, humpback whale, the green sea turtle, dolphins, killer whale, (next page) the seal, walruses, and the river dolphin.*

## Evaluating the Hypothesis

Before testing to see if a hypothesis is true, a scientist tries to think of reasons why it might be false. This process is known as evaluating the hypothesis. This step saves scientists the time, effort, and expense of testing hypotheses that are not likely to be true.

Scientists have found many problems with the hypotheses given above. An important one is that all of the animals discussed so far—whales, porpoises, seals, and sea cows—are rather easy to see in the wild. All of these animals are mammals, which means, among other things, that they breathe air. Even though they swim underwater, they must come to the surface to breathe.

Seals are especially easy to see because they spend a lot of time outside the water, basking in the sun. They also give birth to their pups on land. Seals also make a lot of noise. If

*Walruses are large, noisy, and easily seen. It is hard to believe they could be mistaken for the shy, silent creature Nessie is said to be.*

*Elephant seals are large enough to qualify as small Nessies, but they give birth on land, bask in the sun, and make lots of noise. Could Nessie be an elephant seal?*

seals lived in Loch Ness, people probably would have seen or heard them. No one has ever reported seeing a seal in the lake.

Sea cows are easy to see because they swim slowly. They are not shy of humans, either. Stellar's sea cow became extinct partly because it did not try to hide from the people who hunted it. Nessie, on the other hand, is shy. It swims away quickly whenever it sees a person.

One reason to rule out whales and sea cows is diet. Nearly all whales eat plankton, a simple form of plant and animal life that lives in salt water. Since Loch Ness contains fresh water, it does not have plankton in it. Without plankton, most whales would starve. Sea cows survive by eating large water plants. Because the water in Loch Ness is very cold, it supports very little plant life. A sea cow would starve in Loch Ness.

## Is Nessie a Turtle?

Many scientists doubt that the Loch Ness Monster is a mammal, but they still believe it is some kind of known animal. For example, some scientists have hypothesized that Nessie might be a giant turtle. Turtles have long, slender necks and small heads, like Nessie. Their curved shells could appear as humps in the water. Some turtles grow as large as ten feet long—long enough, scientists argue, to qualify as Nessie.

Since turtles eat fish, they would find plenty to eat in Loch Ness. The icy waters are rich with trout, salmon, pike, and eels. Turtles also can walk on land. If Nessie is a turtle, it would explain why the creature is sometimes seen crossing a road or skidding down a slope toward the water.

One problem with the turtle hypothesis is that the world's known large turtles do not like cold water. This is because turtles are reptiles, which are cold-blooded. Reptiles depend on the environment to warm their bodies. They often lie on sunny rocks to warm themselves. Another problem is that most people have seen a turtle at some time in their lives. It is hard to believe they would confuse a turtle with a monster like Nessie.

*Reptiles and fish are better candidates for Nessie than mammals are, some scientists believe. The giant salamander (top) likes cold freshwater and can remain submerged for long periods of time. The eel (center) also likes cold water and eats many types of matter, living and dead. The eel sometimes swims with its head poking out of the water, as Nessie does. The giant turtle (bottom) has a slender neck and a small head, like Nessie. Its shell could appear like the hump Nessie is said to have.*

## The Case for Giant Salamanders

Roy Mackal, a Nessie researcher, has hypothesized that Nessie is a giant salamander "thought to be extinct for 250 million years." Fossils show that these creatures sometimes grew up to sixteen feet long. In support of his hypothesis, Mackal notes that many creatures once believed to be extinct have been found alive. In 1938, a coelacanth, a fish believed to be extinct for seventy million years, was found in the Indian Ocean off the coast of Africa. In addition, giant meat-eating lizards presently live on Komodo, an island off Indonesia in the Far East. These salamanderlike creatures may grow to ten feet in length and three hundred pounds in weight.

Mackal has strong reasons for believing Nessie is a giant salamander. For one thing, salamanders like cold, fresh water. For another, they eat many things. A salamander would find an endless supply of food in Loch Ness. Salamanders are great swimmers, but they also have legs. They can move around well on land.

The main problem with the salamander hypothesis is one of appearance. Photographs and eyewitness reports of Nessie reveal a creature with a long neck and a small head. A salamander has a short neck and a large head.

## Sleek Eels

A creature that more closely resembles Nessie is a snakelike fish known as the eel. In 1954, a newspaper in Scotland published a story entitled "The Loch Ness Mystery—Is Nessie Really a Giant Eel?" Some types of eel live in fresh water. The sleek creatures like cold water and eat almost anything, living or dead. Eels have been found and caught in Loch Ness. They sometimes swim with their small heads poking out of the water, like Nessie. They have gills, so they can breathe underwater. While they prefer to live in the water, eels can and do travel on land. They have two fins on the front part of their bodies that could be mistaken for flippers.

# Is Loch Ness the Only Lake Containing a Monster?

Strange water beasts have been sighted in lakes around the world. In the 1950s and 1960s, residents around Lake Khaiyr, Lake Vorota, and Lake Labynkyr in Siberia reported seeing huge beasts with long, shiny necks and huge bodies, like Nessie. In 1953, a geologist named V.A. Tverdokhlebov reported seeing a lake creature that "had eyes, light-colored patches on the side of its head, and a dark gray body. Along its back was a twenty-inch high fin. It moved forward in leaps and at 100 yards from shore it stopped and sent up a great cascade of spray before diving out of sight."

Okanagan Lake in western Canada is said to contain a thirty- to seventy-foot-long creature known as Ogopogo. The Native Americans who lived near the lake called the creature Na-ha-ha-itkh. Since white settlers arrived in 1860, Ogopogo has been seen many times. A water skier who got close to the monster reported that it had "blue-gray scales" that "glistened like a rainbow trout as the sun shone on him." Other strange creatures have been reported in Canada's lakes Manitoba, Dauphin, and Winnipegosis.

Strange lake creatures have been sighted in the United States as well. Strange water creatures have been seen in Lake Champlain since 1609. In that year, Samuel de Champlain noted "a serpentine creature twenty feet long, thick as a barrel, with a head like a horse." In 1992, home-made video tapes of a mysterious creature swimming in the lake were shown on the television program *Sightings*. So many people have sighted a creature in Lake Champlain that the beast now has a nickname: Champ.

In 1885, a steamboat captain fired on a whale-sized creature swimming in Flathead Lake in Montana. In 1960, visitors to a country club beside the lake reported seeing an unusual beast rubbing its body against a pier. A woman said, "It was a horrible looking thing with a head about the size of a horse and about a foot of neck showing."

One problem with accepting an eel as Nessie is the size. The longest known eel is only ten feet long. Nessie is much longer. Also, eel bodies are slender. Nessie's neck is slender, but its body is thick. Eels are fast swimmers, but they move by whipping their bodies from side to side. Nessie is described as moving in an up-and-down manner. Still, scientists say that eels sometimes swim on their sides, which would create an up-and-down motion. Side-swimming eels could also appear to have humps.

If the Loch Ness creature is not an eel, perhaps it is a giant sea slug. Sea slugs resemble snails without shells. Some of them have bristles that help them move and head growths that look like feelers or horns. When they move, they hump themselves up and then stretch themselves out something like an earthworm does—and something like many reports say Nessie does. The largest known sea slugs are about two feet long and weigh about fifteen pounds. But it is possible that slugs two or three times this big live in the depths of Loch Ness.

The biggest drawback to the idea of a sea slug being Nessie is that sea slugs do not come out onto land. (There are land slugs as well, but they are generally quite small and they do not live in water like Nessie does.)

## A Creature from the Age of Dinosaurs

The strangest but most intriguing hypothesis is that Nessie is a type of swimming reptile known as a plesiosaur. Plesiosaurs lived at the same time that dinosaurs ruled the land. Scientists believe that, like dinosaurs, plesiosaurs have been extinct for seventy million years. The coelacanth was believed to be extinct for the same amount of time, yet it is very much alive today. Could some plesiosaurs still be living?

Fossils of plesiosaur bones have been found near Loch Ness. These fossils provide the strongest evidence in support of the plesiosaur hypothesis. When scientists fit the fossils together, the skeletons they make reveal a creature that matches Nessie exactly.

Plesiosaurs grew from twenty to fifty feet long—the same size Nessie is said to be. They had long, thin necks and small

heads, just like Nessie. Their bodies were huge, weighing tons. Plesiosaurs had large front and rear flippers. Thanks to these flippers, plesiosaurs could swim very quickly, leaving a wake just as Nessie does. Plesiosaurs were fish eaters, so they could find lots of food in Loch Ness. When they hunted fish, they stretched out their necks, causing their backs to hump up. A plesiosaur seeking food near the surface of the water would appear to have a hump.

Although a living plesiosaur would look a lot like Nessie, the plesiosaur hypothesis has problems, too. For one thing, plesiosaurs did not live in fresh water like that found in Loch Ness. They lived in salt water. Scientists point out, however, that Loch Ness was once filled with salt water. After the lake was cut off from the North Sea, its water slowly became fresh. This change in Loch Ness took thousands of years. Some scientists believe plesiosaurs could have adapted to this slow change.

*An artist's conception of living plesiosaurs shows why these ancient creatures are considered by many to be the ideal candidates for the Loch Ness Monster. Fossilized plesiosaur remains reveal massive creatures with long, slender necks. Could a colony of plesiosaurs live in the lake?*

Plesiosaurs could not breathe underwater. They had to come to the surface for air. Some scientists object to the plesiosaur hypothesis because the sightings of Nessie are too rare for the creature to be an air-breathing animal. Those who support the plesiosaur hypothesis point out that some water animals, like crocodiles, have breathing tubes. These passages enable the creatures to remain mostly underwater as they breathe. Several eyewitnesses have described small horns on Nessie's head. If these were breathing tubes, perhaps Nessie could breathe without being seen.

## The Tully-Monster

A writer named F.W. Holiday has identified one more creature, even older than the plesiosaur, that might be Nessie. This is the Tully-monster, or *Tullimonstrum gregarium*, as scientists call it. Scientists only know Tully-monsters from their fossils. They do not even know if the Tully-monster was a worm or a shellfish or some other unknown kind of species. But they do know that Tully-monsters lived in water and resembled Nessie. They had long, skinny necks; tiny heads; wide, arrow-shaped tails; and two small flipperlike attachments on their sides. The fossils show that Tully-monsters looked very much like the Loch Ness creature described by many witnesses. Holiday says they are the closest match in appearance.

Unfortunately, not all the evidence supports Holiday's idea. The largest Tully-monster fossils show them to be only about fourteen inches long. Also, scientists believe they have been extinct for 350 million years. Still, like the coelacanth, thought to be gone for 70 million years, creatures as old as the Tully-monster have been found alive today. Two of them are the *Vampiroteuthis infernalis* (a fish that looks something like a giant squid) and the *Neopilina galathea* (a shellfish that is part snail and part clam). Both of these show up occasionally in Russian deep-sea fishing nets.

All of these hypotheses have merit, but they all present problems as well. Which, if any, is correct? In the last fifty years, many scientists have traveled to Loch Ness to answer that question.

# CHAPTER 3

# Testing the Hypothesis: What Have Scientists Found in Loch Ness?

Once a scientist has formed a hypothesis, he or she must test it. A scientist needs physical proof, such as a photograph, a body, or a skeleton, to confirm a hypothesis. Scientists knew they had to visit Loch Ness to prove or disprove the many hypotheses about the mysterious creature rumored to live in the lake's inky waters.

The first scientific search for Nessie began in July 1934. Sir Edward Mountain, the chairman of an insurance company, hired twenty townspeople from Inverness, a small city located on Loch Ness. These people were hired as official "Watchers for the Monster." They were given binoculars and cameras and were to watch Loch Ness continuously for signs of an unusual creature. Anyone who was able to photograph Nessie would receive a cash bonus. The team, headed by Capt. James Fraser, reported eleven clear sightings.

One of the observers reported seeing something that was "clearly the monster's head." The description he gave was detailed. "On top of the head were two stumps resembling a sheep's horns broken off," he reported. The creature had slitted eyes and smooth black or dark brown, lizardlike skin. The body was about twenty feet long and had flippers in front. The strange creature swam at a speed of about eight miles per hour. It dived out of sight as soon as it saw the man, leaving a stream of bubbles swirling on the water's surface.

Everyone on Sir Edward's team carried a camera. Several team members tried to take pictures of the strange beast they observed. Due to the darkness of the water and the quickness of the creature, only five pictures were clear. Of these, four showed nothing more than disturbances of the dark water's surface. The fifth seemed to show an object spewing up a jet of mist.

Captain Fraser himself took the first motion pictures of the Loch Ness Monster. Hearing of Fraser's good luck, many people became very excited. The developed film was not very clear, however. Some scientists made fun of Fraser's movie, saying that it showed nothing more than a swimming seal.

## More than a Legend

In 1935, another scientist arrived at Loch Ness to look into the mystery. Her name was Dr. Constance Whyte. From 1935 to 1955, Dr. Whyte collected eyewitness accounts of Nessie sightings from people who lived around Loch Ness. In 1957, Dr. Whyte published the accounts in a book entitled *More than a Legend*.

Excited by Dr. Whyte's book, Tim Dinsdale, an engineer, began to hunt for Nessie in 1960. Using a hand held movie camera, Dinsdale captured the image of a strange creature swimming in Loch Ness. The beast was at least six feet wide and five feet high with a hump at least twelve feet long. "As it proceeded westward," Dinsdale later recalled, "I watched successive rhythmic bursts of foam break the surface." Dinsdale believed that what he saw were the creature's paddle strokes. He said, "I . . . began to count—one, two, three, four—pure white blobs of froth contrasting starkly with the surrounding black water."

Dinsdale's film was studied by photography experts from the British Royal Air Force. They concluded that the movie showed a living thing "that might be anywhere

*The ruined remains of Urquhart Castle overlook the dark waters known for centuries as* Loch na Beiste, *Gaelic for "Lake of the Beast."*

from 30 to 92 feet long" moving through the water at about ten miles per hour.

Other scientists were not convinced that Dinsdale's film showed a live creature. They argued that the object in the water was nothing more than a small motorboat.

Dinsdale's movie was shown on British television, stirring up new interest in Nessie. Four people decided to form a scientific organization devoted to studying the Loch Ness mystery. The founding members called their group the Loch Ness Phenomenon Investigation Bureau (LNPIB). One of the charter members was David James, a former British naval officer and a member of Parliament. Constance Whyte, the author of *More than a Legend*, was another member. The other two charter members were Peter Scott and Richard Fitter. Both men were naturalists, scientists who specialize in the study of plants and animals.

Many people volunteered to help the LNPIB search for Nessie. These volunteers included businesspeople, farmers, housewives, students, and teachers. They carried notepads, movie cameras, and binoculars. They were stationed on boats and on the shore around Loch Ness. Some stayed at the lake from 4:00 A.M. until 10:00 P.M. Great spotlights were shone on the lake after dark. The LNPIB hoped Nessie might be attracted to or curious about the light.

Eventually, the group included enough people to watch as much as 70 percent of the lake at one time. The LNPIB published a newsletter, updating its members on its findings. They posted signs around the lake, asking anyone who seriously thought they had sighted the lake creature to report it to the LNPIB headquarters. But the LNPIB could not provide proof of a strange animal dwelling in the lake.

*Nessie hunter Tim Dinsdale holds the motion picture camera he used to capture the image of a large creature swimming in the loch in 1960. Experts from the British Royal Air Force concluded that Dinsdale's movie showed a living thing.*

# What Is Sonar?

The word *sonar* is short for so(und) na(vigation and) r(anging). As the name suggests, sonar is a device that uses sound to navigate underwater. The device works by making a sound underwater. The sound waves move outward from the device, traveling through the water. When sound waves strike a distant object, they bounce back toward the sonar equipment. By measuring the time it takes for the sound wave to return, the sonar equipment can tell the user how far away the object is, how large it is, and whether or not it is moving. Because the system measures echoes, it is sometimes called an echosounder.

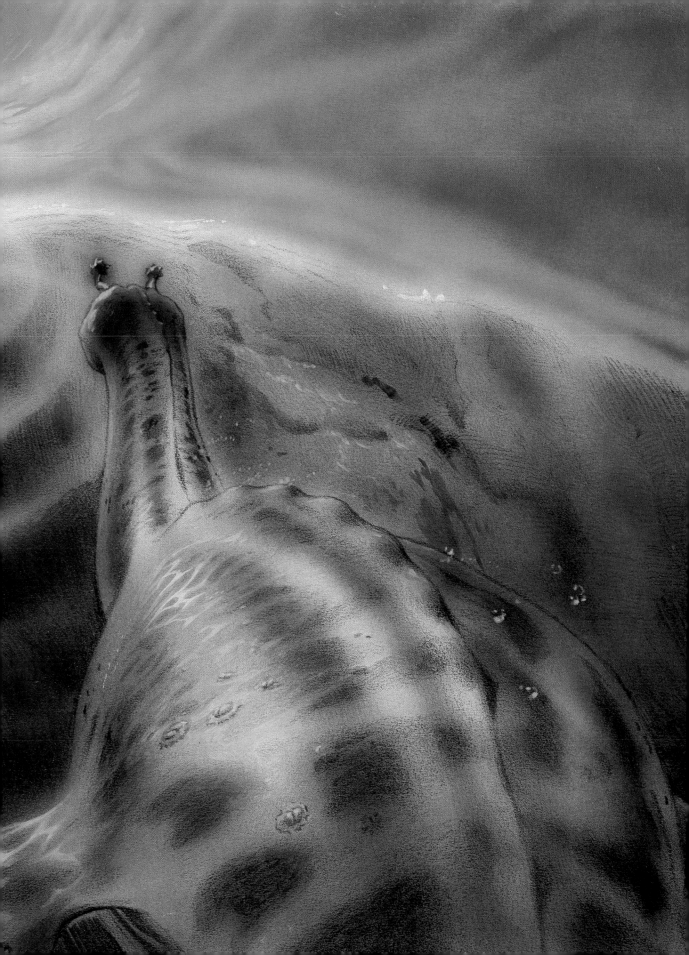

## Searching with Sound

One scientist, named Col. H.G. Hassler, thought the LNPIB was going about its search the wrong way. He believed that the noise from LNPIB motorboats was scaring Nessie. In 1962, Hassler took a sailboat to Loch Ness to search for the elusive creature. He had equipped his boat with underwater listening devices, but he heard nothing unusual in Loch Ness.

In 1967, scientists from the University of Birmingham, England, decided that the best way to locate Nessie would be to use an advanced listening technique known as sonar.

Sonar instruments bounce sound waves off underwater objects. By listening to the "echo" of sound waves, scientists can detect the presence of objects underwater.

Professor D. Gordon Tucker, chairman of the University of Birmingham Department of Electronic and Electrical Engineering, supervised the sonar testing in Loch Ness. He reported that the Birmingham team tracked an object moving near the lake bottom at the speed of 100 feet a minute. A second object was spotted. Then a third. The last one was traveling 450 feet a minute, faster than a salmon or any other fish in the lake could swim. Professor Tucker declared that the sonar results came from "a number of large animate [living] objects." He did not say what kind of animal could be moving so fast at such a great depth.

*Dr. Robert Rines of the Academy of Applied Sciences readies an underwater camera to search for the Loch Ness Monster during the mid-1970s (top). Members of the Loch Ness Phenomenon Investigation Bureau peer across the mysterious waters hoping to glimpse Nessie from an observation platform (center). In a specially outfitted boat, Tim Dinsdale searches for the elusive creature in 1969 (bottom).*

Although his results were very unclear, they were enough to encourage Don Taylor, a scientist from Atlanta, Georgia. Taylor used a small submarine named *Viperfish* to explore the dark loch. Optimistically, Taylor had biopsy harpoons mounted on his submarine. These harpoons would be used to take tissue samples of Nessie, if the creature were sighted. Scientists could then analyze the samples and try to determine exactly what kind of species Nessie came from.

Taylor did sight something on his radar screen. Whatever it was moved too fast for Taylor's little vessel to keep up. And the lake was too murky for him to see anything through the sub's windows. His expedition was a disappointment.

In 1970, also intrigued by Professor Tucker's findings, researchers from the Academy of Applied Sciences, based in Boston, Massachusetts, arrived at Loch Ness. The team, headed by Dr. Robert Rines, the president of the academy, used sonar to map the bottom of Loch Ness. Their survey revealed that the lake is much deeper than previously believed—more than nine hundred feet deep in some places. It also showed a number of underwater caves that might contain air for the creatures living in them to breathe. On September 21, 1970, the sonar scanner recorded two large objects passing through its beam. Unfortunately, the team was not able to determine what these objects might be. Their only conclusion was that the objects did not seem to be fish.

After new reports of these and other disappointing excursions to Loch Ness, many people once again gave up on Nessie. Most thought the creature was a joke—or a dream. But in fact, mysterious sightings continued. The commercial fishing ships that worked the lake reported several unidentified, apparently living, things in the lake. Capt. Alex Knot, for one, said he and his crew had "spotted an underwater animal on more than one trip through the lake." He claimed that on one occasion, they observed a creature for eighteen minutes. "It was at a depth of fifty-two

*Jennifer Bruce, a Canadian tourist, did not see the strange figure in the middle of the lake when she took this picture of Loch Ness in 1982. The curved shape is believed by many to be the neck and head of the Loch Ness Monster.*

feet, moving at six miles per hour, had a length of twenty-four feet, six inches, and was shaped like an eel," he reported.

But once again, no photographs were taken and there was no proof of Nessie except the word of a few observers. This alone was not enough for scientists. They had to try again to find good, sound evidence.

## A Startling Photograph

In 1971, the Academy of Applied Sciences returned to Loch Ness. This time, the members of the academy brought along the most advanced equipment ever used to search for the Loch Ness Monster. They placed a camera underwater and connected it to a strobe, a bright light that flashes for an instant. Both the camera and the strobe were connected to a sonar scanner. The equipment was set up so the sonar scanner would trigger the strobe and the camera when an object passed nearby.

Over and over, salmon, eels, and mackerel triggered the camera. Then, on August 7, 1972, the sonar detected the movement of a large creature far underwater. Within a moment, the underwater strobe flashed four times. The film in the camera recorded four images. These pictures changed forever what many people thought of the Loch Ness Monster.

The photographs show a huge fin jutting out from what appears to be a very large body. Scientists judged the fin to be from six to eight feet long and two to four feet wide. No living creature on earth is known to have fins of such size. There have been creatures with such fins in the past, however. The fin in the photograph looks amazingly like the fin of a plesiosaur.

# Confirming the Tests: Has Any New Evidence of Nessie Been Found?

One of the most important steps of the scientific method is confirmation of earlier test results. Scientists have a saying, "Nothing happens once." In other words, if scientists cannot repeat the results of an experiment, they cannot accept the first findings as scientific fact. They assume that either they made a mistake in their first observation, or some sort of accident occurred.

Since 1972, many attempts have been made to confirm the Academy of Applied Sciences' discovery of a large, unidentified creature in Loch Ness. In 1973, members of the academy returned to the lake. They hoped to obtain more photographs and more sonar readings. Although they searched for months, they found nothing. Many people began to doubt the team's earlier results.

## The Jackpot

Two years later, members of the Academy of Applied Sciences returned to Loch Ness for another try at confirming Nessie's existence. In June 1975, their sonar detected the presence of a massive body moving through the depths of Loch Ness. The academy's powerful strobe lights flashed again and again. The underwater cameras recorded a huge shape that glided, turned, and then disappeared into the water's vast blackness.

Members of the academy rushed their photographs to the National Aeronautics and Space Administration (NASA) in Washington, D.C., for computer enhancement. In this process, computers are used to sharpen the details of an unclear picture.

Some people believe that computer enhancement does not give true results. They claim that the people operating the computers may influence the results, either accidentally or on purpose. Others say this computer technique is a valuable tool.

The results were amazing. One photograph showed what the academy called "the main body structure" of a large water animal. It said the picture showed the animal's head, neck, body, and what appeared to be front flippers.

Another photograph was even more startling. It showed a shape that some scientists thought looked like a head. The head seemed to have slitted eyes, a mouth, and two short tubes on top. The grainy photograph was laughed at by some scientists. Others were struck by the similarity of the photograph to the description given by a member of Captain Fraser's team in 1934. That witness had described a head with "two stumps resembling a sheep's horns broken off." Many people who viewed the photograph believed they were looking at the face of the Loch Ness Monster.

"We've got it," exclaimed Robert Rines, when he viewed the enhanced photographs. "We've hit the jackpot."

Rines's colleague, author Nicholas Witchell, agreed. "The search is over," Witchell declared. He began work on a new book about the Loch Ness Monster. He called the academy's findings "one of the greatest and most dramatic discoveries of the twentieth century."

## The Wonder of Ness

Believing he had discovered a new species of animal, Dr. Rines made up a name for the creature he had photographed. He called it *Nessitera rhombopteryx*. The name is Latin for "wonder of Ness with the diamond-shaped fin."

Many scientists shared Rines's and Witchell's excitement. After examining the academy's pictures and sonar readings, Dr. George Zug of the Smithsonian Institution in Washington, D.C., expressed support for Rines's findings. Zug said that he believed the large objects recorded by the academy were "the recently described *Nessitera rhombopteryx,* previously known as the Loch Ness monsters."

*Members of the Academy of Applied Sciences lower an underwater camera into the inky depths of Loch Ness. Dr. Robert Rines, the head of the team, stands at right.*

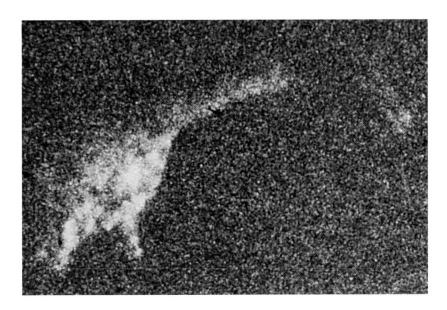

*An underwater photograph taken in 1975 by the Academy of Applied Sciences shows "the main body structure" of a large water animal.*

Dr. Christopher McGowen, associate curator of Toronto's Royal Ontario Museum in Canada, agreed. "I am satisfied that there is sufficient weight of evidence to support that there is an unexplained phenomenon of considerable interest in Loch Ness," he said. "The evidence suggests the presence of large aquatic animals."

Other scientists remained doubtful, however. Zoologists from London's Natural History Museum pointed out that the process of enhancing a photograph with a computer can distort an image. In the opinion of these scientists, the chances for error were too great to say for certain that the photographs showed a living creature. "We believe that none of the 1975 photographs is sufficiently informative to prove the existence, far less the identity of a large, living animal," the staff of scientists concluded.

The Natural History Museum scientists suggested that the academy's photographs showed "a large number of small gas bubbles such as are found in the sacks of phantom midges." Midges are gnatlike insects that are known to move underwater in large swarms.

Many reporters also doubted the findings. Some thought that perhaps the underwater cameras had photographed a sunken Viking ship. Others wondered if the team from the academy had accidentally photographed a life-size model of the Loch Ness Monster that was lost in the lake during the making

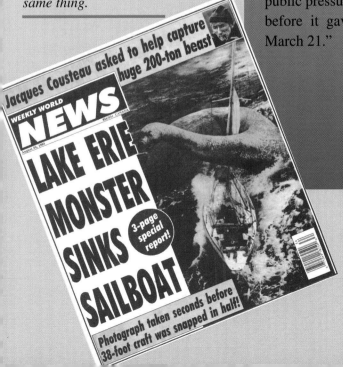

*Nessie's frequent appearance on the covers of tabloid newspapers is proof of the ongoing fascination with "the wonder of Ness." The publishers of the weekly newspapers have found that their sales rise and fall dramatically, depending on the subject matter of the covers. When publishers find a topic that sells well—such as the capture of the Loch Ness Monster—they are quick to follow up with more stories about the same thing.*

# Has Nessie Been Captured?

On January 14, 1992, the front-page headline of the tabloid newspaper *Weekly World News* declared, "Loch Ness Monster Captured!" According to the story, written by Zack Hagar, "Scientists from seven countries trapped the Loch Ness monster in a steel net baited with tuna fish on December 22." Two photographs appeared with the story, each showing a dinosaurlike creature swimming with a scuba diver. According to the report, a French zoologist, Dr. Michel Genet, organized the "3-year, $9 million research project." Dr. Genet was quoted as saying, "This is it. This is the proof we have been waiting for."

Was the capture real? The major news organizations did not think so. The story was not picked up by newswire services such as the Associated Press, nor did it appear on television or in any daily newspapers. No serious Nessie seekers were invited to view the beast before it was reportedly released. The photographs did not appear genuine, either. In one, the monster's head appears near the camera with its body and tail in the background. If the picture were taken in the murky waters of Loch Ness, as reported, such distant details would not be visible.

Undaunted, *Weekly World News* reported on April 14, 1992, "Loch Ness Monster Has a Baby!" In another story, Zack Hagar wrote, "Scientists who captured and threatened to murder the Loch Ness monster earlier this year bowed to public pressure and released the pregnant creature just hours before it gave birth to a 2,000-pound baby monster on March 21."

of the 1969 movie *The Private Life of Sherlock Holmes.* These theories did not explain the movements recorded by the sonar equipment that tripped the cameras, but many skeptics believed them anyway. "Nessie, This Is Your Best Show Yet" mocked a headline in the *Sunday Times* of London.

## More Evidence?

Confident that they could confirm their findings to the satisfaction of all, the Academy of Applied Sciences returned to Loch Ness in 1976. Aided by money from the *New York Times*, the academy set up six underwater cameras. Four cameras would take still pictures when triggered by sonar readings. Three of these cameras used 35-millimeter film that needed to be developed in a film laboratory. The fourth camera, a Polaroid SX-70 camera, would take pictures that could be viewed instantly. Meanwhile another camera, known as an elapsed-time camera, would take still pictures at regular intervals. The sixth camera was a television camera. Every sixteen seconds a giant strobe lit up the murky depths of Loch Ness for the elapsed-time camera and the television camera. The academy took 108,000 pictures. None contained anything that resembled Nessie.

The academy returned again in 1979. This time, the scientists rigged sonar-triggered cameras and strobe lights to three trained dolphins. The dolphins swam the depths of Loch Ness, but no photographs of Nessie were taken. The experiment was cut short when one of the dolphins died.

In October 1987, about twenty-four motorboats outfitted with sonar equipment sailed across Loch Ness side by side, sweeping the waters for evidence of the legendary creature. Something large did show up at the depth of six hundred feet. "No one here was prepared to say it was the Loch Ness Monster," wrote a reporter for the *Washington Post*, "but few would swear it wasn't."

*"We've got it," exclaimed Nessie hunter Dr. Robert Rines when he saw the photograph taken in June 1975 (below). Rines declared that the computer-enhanced image showed the head of the Loch Ness Monster. Skeptics scoffed at the claim. Some suggested that the head belonged to a model of the Loch Ness Monster that was lost during the filming of the 1969 motion picture* The Private Life of Sherlock Holmes *(above).*

# The Search Continues

A great deal of evidence—photographs, movie film, and sonar readings—supports the hypothesis that a large, unidentified aquatic animal lives in Loch Ness. Still, some scientists continue to wait for hard evidence—a body, a bone, even a tooth. Until one of these things is found, these skeptics will not accept the notion that an unusual creature exists in Loch Ness. So far, no such proof has turned up.

Scientists continue to probe the depths of Loch Ness searching for the legendary beast. Many are convinced that it is just a matter of time before they produce proof positive that Nessie exists. Others remain skeptical.

Meanwhile, millions of people around the world wait for further word about the great creature. Many of these people hope the question will not be settled during their lifetimes. They enjoy the thought that something wonderful and strange lives in the world, beyond the reach of science. For these people, Nessie is like the mystery of life itself, destined to remain forever unsolved.

*Anthony Shiels took this photograph at Loch Ness on May 21, 1977. Is this the Loch Ness Monster?*

# Glossary

**aquatic:** Living in water.

**biographer:** A person who writes an account of another person's life.

**biologist:** A scientist who studies living things.

**computer enhancement:** A technique used to make photographs appear clearer. Critics say this process can distort, or change, an image greatly.

**controversy:** A dispute or debate.

**curator:** A person in charge of a museum.

**evaluate:** To determine the worth of; to appraise.

**exhibition:** A collection of objects put on display.

**extinct:** No longer existing; having no living successors.

**flipper:** A wide, flat limb adapted for swimming.

**hypothesis:** An unproved scientific conclusion drawn from known facts. A hypothesis is used as a basis for further investigation or experimentation.

**mammal:** A warm-blooded animal that breathes air, has hair, gives birth to live young, and nurses its babies.

***Nessitera rhombopteryx*:** A scientific name for the creature photographed in Loch Ness by the Academy of Applied Sciences. *Nessitera* combines the name of the lake, *Ness*, with the Greek word *teras*, meaning "wonder" or "monster." *Rhombopteryx* combines the Greek word *rhombos*, meaning "diamond shape," with *pteryx*, meaning "fin" or "wing." Together, the name translates as "the wonder of Ness with the diamond-shaped fin."

**paleontologist:** A scientist who uses fossils to study ancient life forms.

**reptile:** A cold-blooded animal that breathes air and usually is covered with scales or horny plates.

**sonar:** A device that uses underwater sound waves for navigation, range finding, or detection of submerged objects.

**strobe light:** An electron tube that produces short, bright flashes of light.

**theory:** An arrangement of facts that explains a phenomenon.

**zoology:** The study of the structure, development, and functions of animals.

# For Further Reading

Elwood D. Baumann, *The Loch Ness Monster.* New York: Franklin Watts, 1972.

Janet Bord and Colin Bord, *Alien Animals.* Harrisburg, PA: Stackpole, 1981.

Daniel Cohen, *The Encyclopedia of Monsters.* New York: Dodd, Mead & Company, 1982.

John Godwin, *This Baffling World.* New York: Hart Publishing, 1968.

Patricia Lauber, *Mystery Monsters of Loch Ness.* Champaign, IL: Garrard Publishing, 1978.

Ellen Rabinowich, *The Loch Ness Monster.* New York: Franklin Watts, 1979.

# Works Consulted

Henry H. Bauer, *The Enigma of Loch Ness.* Chicago: University of Illinois Press, 1986.

*Chicago Tribune*, "Fishy Form Detected in Search for 'Nessie,'" October 13, 1987.

Bernard Heuvelmans, *In the Wake of the Sea-Serpents.* New York: Hill and Wang, 1968.

Tyler Marshall, "Loch Ness Monster Search Will Try More High Tech," *Los Angeles Times*, October 4, 1987.

——— , "Sonar Fails to Solve Loch Ness Mystery," *Los Angeles Times*, October 12, 1987.

Robert D. San Souci, *The Loch Ness Monster.* San Diego: Greenhaven Press, 1989.

# Index

Academy of Applied Sciences, 34-37, 42
Adamnan, Saint, 5

Boyd, Alastair, 15
British Museum of Natural History, 13
British Royal Air Force, 30-31
Bruce, Jennifer, 35

Campbell, Alex, 8
Champlain, Samuel de, 24
coelacanth, 23, 26, 28
Columba, Saint, 5, 7
computer enhancement, 37-38, 42
crocodile, 28

*Daily Mail*, 13, 15-16
Dinsdale, Tim, 30-31, 34

echosonar. *See* sonar
Edinburgh College, 14
eel, 23, 26
elephant seal, 17

Fraser, James, 29-30

Genet, Michel, 41
Grant, Arthur, 14-15, 18
Gray, Hugh, 12-13

Hagar, Zack, 41
Hassler, H.G., 34
Holiday, F.W., 28
humpback whale, 17
hypothesis, 17

*Inverness Courier*, 8

Knot, Alex, 35-36

Lake of the Beast (*Loch na Beiste*), 7
LNPIB (Loch Ness Phenomenon Investigation Bureau), 31, 34
*Loch na Beiste* (Lake of the Beast), 7
Loch Ness
    as good place to hide, 10
    location and map, 9

Loch Ness Monster (Nessie)
    captured?, 40-41
    earliest reported sighting, 5
    first photographic evidence, 12-13
    search continues, 43
    what it could be
        eel, 23, 26
        giant salamander, 22-23
        plesiosaur, 26-28, 36
        porpoise, 17
        sea cow, 19, 21
        seal, 17-18, 20-21
        sea lion, 19
        sea slug, 26
        Tully-monster, 28
        turtle, 19, 21-22
        walrus, 18
        whale, 17, 21
Loch Ness Phenomenon Investigation Bureau (LNPIB), 31, 34

Mackal, Roy, 6, 23
Mackay, John, 8
Mackay, Mrs. John, 8
Martin, David, 15
McGowen, Christopher, 39
Mocumin, Lugne, 5
*More than a Legend* (Whyte), 30-31
Mountain, Sir Edward, 29

Na-ha-ha-itkh (creature), 24
National Aeronautics and Space Administration (NASA), 37
Natural History Museum (London), 39
*Neopilina galathea*, 28
Nessie. *See* Loch Ness Monster
*Nessitera rhombopteryx*, 38
*New York Times*, 42

Ogopogo (creature), 24

peat, 5, 10
phantom midges, 39
plesiosaur, 26-28, 36
porpoise, 17
    river dolphin, 19

*The Private Life of Sherlock Holmes* (movie), 42

Rines, Robert, 34, 38, 42
Royal Ontario Museum, 39

salamander, giant, 22-23
scientific method
    steps of, 6
sea cow, 19, 21
    Stellar's, 19
seal, 17-18, 20-21
    elephant, 17, 21
sea lion, 19
sea slug, 26
Shiels, Anthony, 43
*Sightings* (TV program), 24
Smithsonian Institution, 38
sonar
    as search device, 34-35
    what it is, 32
Spicer, George, 9
Spicer, Mrs. George, 9
Spurling, Christian, 15
*Sunday Times* (London), 42

tabloid newspapers, 40-41
Taylor, Don, 35
Tucker, D. Gordon, 34
Tully-monster (*Tullimonstrum gregarium*), 28
turtle, 19, 21-22
Tverdokhlebov, V.A., 24

*Vampiroterthis infernalis*, 28
*Viperfish* (submarine), 35

walrus, 18, 20
*Washington Post*, 42
*Weekly World News*, 41
Wetherell, Marmaduke, 13, 15-16
whale, 17
    humpback, 17
Whyte, Constance, 30
Wilson, Robert, 15-16
Witchell, Nicholas, 38

Zug, George, 38

# About the Author

Bradley Steffens lives in Poway, California, with his children, Ezekiel and Tessa. He is the author of ten nonfiction books for young people, including *Free Speech*; *The Children's Crusade*; *Phonograph: Sound on Disk*; *Photography: Preserving the Past*; and *Printing Press: Ideas into Type*.

Mr. Steffens also is a widely published poet and playwright. His poetry and plays are filled with wondrous creatures—angels, giants, space aliens, a centaur, a satyr, a talking fig tree, and a twelve-foot-long iguana. He takes as a motto for his life and work a verse by the great American poet, Emily Dickinson: "I dwell in possibility."

# Picture Credits

DEMCO